Who is Pooing in My Garden?

A book about animals, insects, and poo!

P N Burrows

Who is Pooing in My Garden?

First published in 2024

Copyright © P N Burrows 2024

The rights of the author have been asserted in accordance with Sections 77 and 78 of the Copyright Designs and Patents Act, 1988. All rights reserved.

No part of this book may be reproduced (including photocopying or storing in any medium by electronic means and whether or not transiently or incidentally to some other use of this publication) without the written permission of the copyright holder except in accordance with the provisions of the Copyright, design and Patents Act 1988. Applications for the Copyright holder's written permission to reproduce any part of this publication should be addresses to the publishers.

Contents

Introduction	1
Four Legged	
Badger	4
Cat	6
Fox	8
Frog	10
Hedgehog	12
Mole	14
Mouse	16
Newt	18
Rabbit	20
Rat	22
Squirrel	24
Toad	26
Creepy-Crawlies	
Ant	30

Beetle	32
Centipede	34
Millipede	36
Spider	38

Slimies

Slug	42
Snail	44
Snake	46
Worm	48

Winged

Bat	52
Bee	54
Blackbird	56
Butterfly	58
Corvid	60
Damselfly	62
Dragonfly	64
Dunnock	66
Fly	68
Ladybird	70
Mayfly	72

Moth	74
Owl	76
Pigeon	78
Robin	80
Sparrow	82
Starling	84
Thrush	86
Tit	88
Wasp	90
Wren	92
Useful Words	94
Helping Wildlife	97
Acknowledgements	99
About the Author	100
Also By	102

Introduction

Introduction

This book is a light-hearted look at the wildlife in British gardens. In it, we'll look at the useful functions that insects and animals play, and we'll talk a lot about animal poo! Who doesn't love talking about poo? I also wrote this book so we could learn a little about the things that scurry, slither, hop, run, and fly about our gardens.

British wildlife is full of beautiful animals and insects. You'll be amazed at how many of them are pooing in your garden!

Without poo, our plants would not grow.

In nature, plants use the energy from the sun to grow, and without insects and animals eating the plants, they would grow out of control. The plant-eating creatures poo out their waste, and this poo makes excellent food for the plants. The cycle continues, with even more plants growing, feeding more insects and animals, who produce even more poo. Your garden is full of poo!

Did you know that the poo from cows and pigs is runny because of the artificial diet fed to them by the farmers? In the wild, their poo is lumpy like that of horses. Pig poo is the smelliest, and it's difficult for farmers to wash the stink out of their clothes.

Manure is a fancy name for animal poo that is used to feed plants. Gardeners scatter manure on the ground next to a plant using a garden fork and gloves. Manure is normally the poo from plant-eating animals (herbivores) like horses, cows, and farm pigs (in the wild, pigs will eat anything).

Poo from meat-eating animals (carnivores) like cats, dogs, and humans is nasty stuff. It takes special insects to digest carnivore poo and turn it into manure.

Nature is amazing, but it is also a little scary. There is always something bigger wanting to eat you. Imagine a mouse scampering across a field, darting from hedge to hedge looking for a bite to eat. The mouse knows there are meat-eating creatures about (predators) that are also looking for their dinner, and so the mouse must be wary not to become their next meal.

Even though we talk a lot about animal poo in this book, please do not play with it or touch it. It will make you ill.

Four Legged

Badger

Badgers are one of the UK's most recognised members of wildlife. They are social animals with extended families living in burrows called 'setts'. They live in a large sett but also have smaller emergency setts scattered about in case they need to flee from predators.

> A long time ago, we didn't have flushing toilets. How would you feel if, like badgers, you had to dig a hole to poo in?

Where do they sleep? Badgers sleep in their setts. They will take grass, straw, and leaves into them to make a bed.

When are they active? Badgers are nocturnal, as they are active at night.

What do they eat? 80% of their diet is earthworms, but they will eat meat, birds, eggs, fruit, and vegetables.

How long do they live for? On average, badgers live for 3 years, but they can live as long as 15 years.

How are they born? 1–5 cubs are born in the sett, and they will spend the first 8 weeks of their life underground.

What are they useful for? Badgers spread undigested seeds in their poo.

Miscellaneous: Badgers pass down setts from one generation to another, and they can have many rooms and up to 50 entrances. Some setts are over 100 years old.

Collective noun: A group of badgers is called a 'cete' or a 'clan'.

Poo Fact

Badgers dig large holes to poo in; these are called 'latrines'. The latrines surround the sett and are used to mark the badger's territory.

Cat

Cats are super cute and cuddly. Who doesn't like cats? Domestic and feral cats are the biggest killer of wildlife in the UK; they are efficient predators. Feral cats are sometimes domestic cats who have run away. They breed in the wild, and the homeless cat cycle continues. Without owners to look after them, domestic cats become wild.

Where do they sleep? Feral cats will always find a safe place to sleep. Like domestic cats, they like to sleep in boxes. Cats can sleep up to 18 hours a day.

When are they active? Cats are most active at dusk and dawn.

What do they eat? Cats are meat eaters, and they cannot digest plants. Feral cats will eat anything they can find, preferably rodents, birds, fish, and insects. Domestic cats eat tinned cat food and biscuits, which provide a carefully balanced diet for them.

Cats are lactose intolerant; this means that milk is bad for them and will make them poorly.

How long do they live for? A typical lifespan of a domestic cat is 12–18 years. Feral cats do not live as long because of the harsher living conditions.

How are they born? 4–12 kittens will be born in a safe environment. A kitten can fend for itself at 12–14 weeks.

What are they useful for? Cats are great at catching rodents, such as rats and mice, but they are equally good at catching birds. Domestic cats make brilliant companions and are fun to have in your life.

Miscellaneous: In 1963, French scientists sent a cat called Félicette into space and brought her back safely.

Collective noun: A group of cats is called a 'clowder'; a group of kittens is a 'kindle'.

Poo Fact

With cats being meat eaters, their poo is vile and of no use to your garden. It has to be eaten by maggots and insects before the plants can use it as food.

Fox

Foxes are very sociable animals. Instead of woofing like a dog, foxes screech and whine. They also tend to be a bit smelly. Foxes can compete with badgers for food, but they are also known to live alongside one another in the badger burrow, which is called a 'sett'. A lot of foxes have moved into towns and cities where food can be found in our bins.

> Would you enjoy having a big fluffy tail?

Where do they sleep? Foxes do not generally sleep in their burrow, which is called a den. They prefer to sleep under bushes or in tall grass.

When are they active? Foxes are nocturnal, preferring to move around at night, but when they are raising cubs, they must forage for food in the daytime, too.

What do they eat? Foxes will eat almost anything, from worms to rabbits, and even fruit and vegetables.

How long do they live for? On average, they live for 1–3 years, but they can reach 9 years old.

How are they born? A mother fox will give birth to 4–5 babies, called cubs. They grow up in the den. After a year, they will either stay with the family to help with the next batch of cubs or move out to form their own dens.

What are they useful for? Foxes help to control the numbers of rodents, pigeons, and rabbits.

Miscellaneous: Even though foxes are members of the dog family, they can retract their claws like cats. Foxes wee on everything to say to other foxes that this area or item is theirs.

Collective noun: A group of foxes is called an 'earth', 'leash', or 'skulk'.

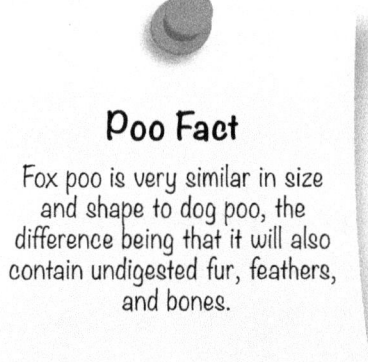

Poo Fact

Fox poo is very similar in size and shape to dog poo, the difference being that it will also contain undigested fur, feathers, and bones.

Frog

There are two types of frog in the UK: the common frog and the northern pool frog. Frogs have been around since the dinosaurs. Frogs and toads are often mistaken for each other. Frogs have smooth, moist skin, and toads have dry, bumpy-looking skin. Both are excellent swimmers and are great for the garden. Frogs have a long, sticky tongue, which is a third of their size, and they flick it out to catch passing insects. They only have teeth on their upper jaw; this prevents them biting their tongue.

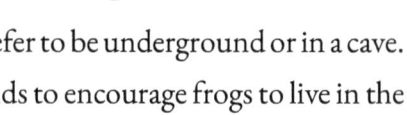

Would you like to flick your tongue out to snatch your food off your plate?

Where do they sleep? They prefer to be underground or in a cave. Gardeners lay clay pots near ponds to encourage frogs to live in the garden.

When are they active? Frogs are most active at night and during dusk.

What do they eat? Flies, worms, snails, and slugs.

How long do they live for? Frogs live for 5–10 years.

How are they born? Frogs will lay hundreds of eggs in a pond; this is called frogspawn. Frogs will lay the eggs in clusters, and the mass has a jelly-like appearance. Because of predators, only 1 in 50 eggs will survive. After 1–3 weeks, a tadpole will emerge from each surviving egg, and over a 14-week period, it changes into a frog.

What are they useful for? They eat a lot of bugs and slugs.

Miscellaneous: Some species of frogs can survive freezing nearly solid in the winter. Frogs can jump 20 times the height of their body, and they can breathe through their skin.

Collective noun: A group of frogs is called an 'army'.

Poo Fact
Adult frogs only poo once a week, and it is huge, measuring a quarter of the size of the frog's body.

Hedgehog

Hedgehogs are another firm favourite in the UK. These cute, spiny creatures got their name due to living in hedges and because they snort like a pig. Prior to this, they were called urchins. They are solitary creatures, preferring to live alone and forage alone. They can walk up to 2 miles in a night and are excellent climbers.

> Can you think of a better name for the hedgehog? Spikey-pig...or maybe hedge-conker?

Where do they sleep? Hedgehogs will sleep in the cover of hedges and bushes. They also make nests to hibernate (sleep) in during the winter months. They will wake up and move nests, so if you leave food out for hedgehogs in the summer, you should also leave some out in winter.

When are they active? Hedgehogs are most active at night.

What do they eat? Hedgehogs will eat most things, but their favourites are worms, snails, slugs, eggs, insects, and fruit. They are lactose intolerant; this means that milk is bad for them and will make them poorly.

How long do they live for? Due to roads and predators, hedgehogs have an average lifespan of 1–2 years, but in a safe environment, they can live for 5–10 years.

How are they born? Around June, a hedgehog will birth 4–5 babies, called hoglets. After 3 weeks, the hoglets will leave the nest and forage with their mother for food, leaving their mother completely a month later.

What are they useful for? They eat a lot of garden pests, such as bugs and slugs.

Miscellaneous: Hedgehogs have many regional names, such as hedgepig, urchin, furze-pig and grainneog.

Collective noun: A group of hedgehogs is called an 'array'.

Poo Fact

The action of running normally causes a hedgehog to poo, and if it is startled by something, it will also poo.

Mole

Moles are creatures that we seldom see in real life. They live underground, digging through the soil creating tunnels, some of them stretching hundreds of metres. Gardeners dislike moles because they disturb the surface of the soil, leaving huge mounds. Their tunnels can also leave plant roots dry, causing the plants to wither.

> Tonight, when you are in bed, you could pretend to be a mole tunnelling underground.

Where do they sleep? Moles sleep in their tunnels.

What do they eat? Mainly worms, but they will eat underground insects and larvae.

How long do they live for? Normally 3 years, but they can live for 5 years.

How are they born? Moles will typically give birth to 3–4 babies. After 6 weeks, they are old enough to look after themselves.

What are they useful for? They eat the larvae of plant-eating bugs. Their tunnels also help excess water to drain away when it rains.

Miscellaneous: Moles can smell in stereo, meaning they know if the scent has come from the left or the right. This helps them locate worms as they drop into the mole's tunnels.

Collective noun: A group of moles is called a 'labour'.

Random Poo Fact
Sloths only poo once a week. They climb down their tree and waggle their bums.

Mouse

There are 6 species of mice in the UK: house mouse, wood mouse, harvest mouse, yellow-necked mouse, hazel mouse, and the edible mouse. With their big eyes, huge ears, and furry coats, mice look really cute, but you would not want a wild one loose in your home. Mice, like rats, have no bladder control and trickle wee as they run.

Would you like to have whiskers like a mouse?

Where do they sleep? Mice sleep in their nests. Depending on species, this could be burrows, hedges, vegetation, sheds, etc.

When are they active? Mice are nocturnal creatures, preferring to come out at night.

What do they eat? Preferring grains, fruits, insects, and seeds, mice will eat almost anything from fruit to dead animals.

How long do they live for? Because of predators, mice rarely live longer than 1 year. If safe, they will live for 3–5 years.

How are they born? 4–7 babies are born in their nest. After 21 days, the mice are old enough to leave, and at 3 months old, they are old enough to breed.

What are they useful for? Mice eat a lot of bugs; a large variety of predators eat them.

Miscellaneous: Mice, like rats, have teeth that constantly grow and need to be worn down by gnawing on things.

Collective noun: A group of mice is called a 'nest'.

Random Poo Fact
Some vultures poo on their own feet to clean them!

Newt

There are three native newt species in the UK: the palmate newt, smooth newt, and the great crested newt. The smooth newt is the most common, and because of declining numbers, the great crested newt is protected by UK law. Even putting a photo of one on social media will get you into serious trouble, as it could attract people to their location.

Like frogs and toads, they are semi-aquatic amphibians, meaning they live on land and in the water.

Would growing up in a pond be fun?

Where do they sleep? Under rocks and in compost heaps.

When are they active? Newts are nocturnal, preferring to move around at night.

What do they eat? Frogspawn, tadpoles, slugs, snails, and insects.

How long do they live for? Up to 17 years.

How are they born? In ponds, newts lay their eggs individually and wrap them up in plant leaves. A newt can lay up to 200 eggs in one session. After 4 weeks, tadpoles will emerge, and they take a further 12–15 weeks to develop enough to leave the pond.

What are they useful for? They eat a lot of bugs.

Miscellaneous: Newts can regrow legs and tails.

Collective noun: A group of newts is called an 'armada'.

Random Poo Fact

The parrot fish munches on algae and the coral that it grows on. It then poos white sand!

Rabbit

The Romans brought rabbits to the UK and farmed them for their meat and fur. In the wild, these fluffy animals reproduce at an alarming rate. Predators such as foxes and hawks reduce their numbers; otherwise, they would multiply beyond the ability of their food to grow. They are social creatures and live in large families. For protection, they dig and live in extensive tunnels called a 'warren'.

Would you like floppy ears and fur like a rabbit?

Where do they sleep? In their warren.

When are they active? People often see rabbits during the day, but they prefer to be out at dusk and dawn.

What do they eat? Rabbits do not really eat carrots; they prefer leafy plants.

How long do they live for? Because of predators, the average is 1–2 years. In a safe environment, they can live up to 9 years.

How are they born? 3–7 babies are born; at 4 months, they can breed themselves. A female, which is called a 'doe', can produce 7 babies every month.

What are they useful for? In the wild, rabbits keep the plants in check. By eating them, they prevent them from becoming too large. Many predators, including humans, eat rabbits.

Miscellaneous: A rabbit's eyes are positioned in a way that enables them to see behind them. Like mice and rats, their teeth keep on growing and they must gnaw at things to keep them short.

Collective noun: A group of rabbits is called a 'colony'.

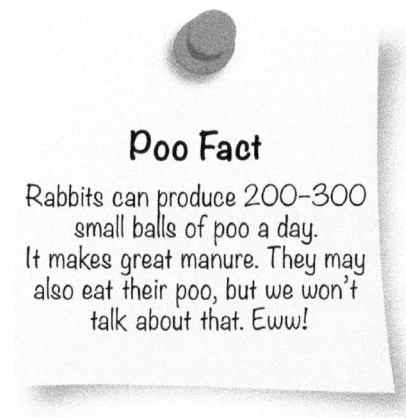

Poo Fact
Rabbits can produce 200–300 small balls of poo a day. It makes great manure. They may also eat their poo, but we won't talk about that. Eww!

Rat

There are two species of rat in the UK, the brown rat and the less common black rat. Ships coming from overseas brought rats to the UK in the 1700s. Brown rats live underground in large colonies. Black rats live in large buildings such as warehouses. Humans should avoid wild rats, as they carry deadly diseases. Rats, like mice, cannot control their bladder and trickle disease-infected wee on everything they walk over. Domestic rats make intelligent and friendly pets.

How would you cope if you had to use the toilet 40 times a day?

Where do they sleep? Like mice, rats like cool, dark, dry places.

When are they active? Rats are nocturnal creatures, preferring to come out at night.

What do they eat? Preferring grains, fruits, insects, and seed, they will eat anything they can find including dead animals.

How long do they live for? Because of predators, rats normally live for 2–3 years. They can live up to 5 years.

How are they born? Up to 20 babies called 'pinkies' are born in their nest. At 5–9 weeks, they leave, and at 6–12 weeks, they are old enough to breed.

What are they useful for? Rats eat a lot of garbage, and a large variety of prey animals feed upon them.

Miscellaneous: Rats are very intelligent with excellent memories. In scientific tests, they solved and remembered the solution to mazes. Like mice, their teeth keep on growing. Rats can gnaw through concrete.

Collective noun: A group of rats is called a 'mischief'.

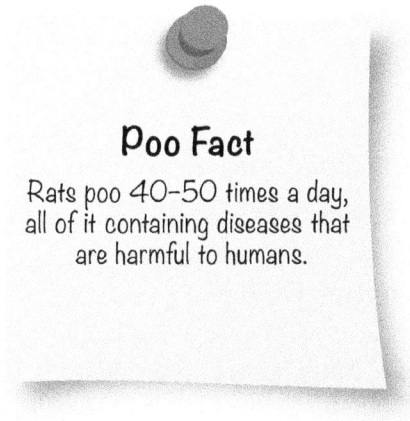

Poo Fact

Rats poo 40–50 times a day, all of it containing diseases that are harmful to humans.

Squirrel

There are two types of squirrel in the UK: the red squirrel and the grey squirrel. Grey squirrels were introduced to the UK in the 1800s, and they are pushing the red squirrel out. Greys will raid the food stores hidden by the red squirrels; they also carry a disease that kills red squirrels. The red squirrels are declining in numbers and can only be found in Formby on Merseyside, the Isle of Wight, the pine forest of Northumberland, Cumbria, and parts of Scotland.

> After burying your food, would you still want to eat it? Eww, it would have worms in it!

Where do they sleep? Squirrels live in trees. Their nests are known as dreys and look like messy balls of sticks, moss, and leaves.

When are they active? Daytime.

What do they eat? Nuts, acorns, and tree seeds. Greys will collect and bury these to eat in winter. The reds will create large stores.

How long do they live for? Life is short for squirrels, as there are many predators that will hunt them. Typically, they will live for 2–5 years.

How are they born? 2–4 babies are born; they are called kits or kittens.

What are they useful for? Grey squirrels bury nuts and seeds. They do not always remember where they put them, and so the nuts and seeds grow.

Miscellaneous: Squirrels have eyes positioned to allow them to see behind them. Their back legs are double-jointed, and their ankles can turn to point their feet forward or backward. This allows them to run up and down trees with ease.

Collective noun: A group of squirrels is called a 'scurry'.

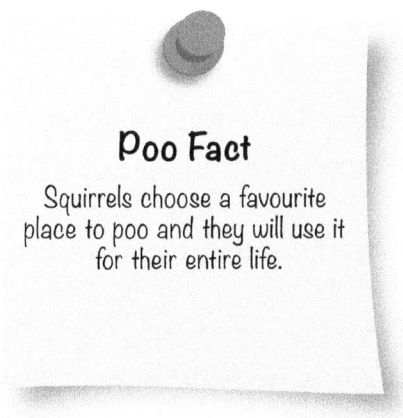

Poo Fact
Squirrels choose a favourite place to poo and they will use it for their entire life.

Toad

There are two types of toad in the UK: the common toad and the natterjack toad. Like frogs, they are excellent swimmers. Natterjack toads are declining in numbers and can only be found in a few places in the UK–the Merseyside coastline, the Cumbrian coast and on the Scottish Solway. Toads prefer to walk rather than hop like frogs. Unlike frogs, toads do not have teeth; they swallow their food whole.

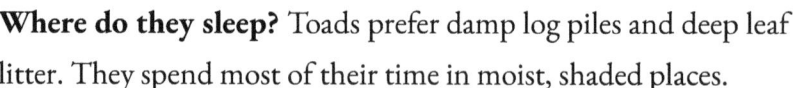

How would you eat without teeth? Yikes, do you clean your teeth twice a day, or you could end up like the toad.

Where do they sleep? Toads prefer damp log piles and deep leaf litter. They spend most of their time in moist, shaded places.

When are they active? Toads are most active at night and during dusk.

What do they eat? Flies, worms, snails, and slugs.

How long do they live for? Average lifespan is 4 years. Some toad species can live between 20–40 years.

How are they born? Toads will lay 1,000–1,500 eggs, called toad-spawn, in a pond. Toads lay the eggs in long strings, and like frog spawn, they have a jelly-like appearance. Because of predators, only 1 in 50 eggs will survive. After 10 days, a tadpole, sometimes called a polliwog, will emerge from each surviving egg, and over a 16-week period, it changes into a toad.

What are they useful for? They eat a lot of bugs.

Miscellaneous: When spooked, toads will release a smelly, foul-tasting liquid from the warts on their backs.

Collective noun: A group of toads is called a 'knot'.

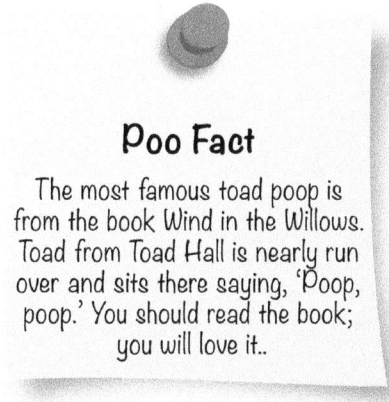

Poo Fact
The most famous toad poop is from the book Wind in the Willows. Toad from Toad Hall is nearly run over and sits there saying, 'Poop, poop.' You should read the book; you will love it..

Creepy-Crawlies

Ant

Ants live in underground communities where every ant has a role to play. Most species are gardeners' friends, as they eat bugs such as greenfly and aphids (pesky bugs that suck the juice out of plants), although some species protect and nurture these sap-sucking aphids, as they produce a liquid called honeydew. It's a little like humans protecting and nurturing cows for their milk (we call this farming). Ants are very intelligent.

Would you like to have thousands of brothers and sisters?

Where do they sleep? Most choose to live in underground nests.

When are they active? Depending on the species, some are active at night and others in the day.

What do they eat? Insects, plants, nectar, and honeydew.

How long do they live for? Worker ants typically live for 3 months, while a queen can last 3–20 years, depending on the species.

How are they born? Larvae are born from eggs. Worker ants care for them until they form cocoons and change into ants.

What are they useful for? They eat a lot of bugs that harm our plants.

Miscellaneous: Once a year, flying queens and males emerge to form new colonies. Queen ants can sleep for up to 9 hours a day, while worker ants have to make do with power naps!

Collective noun: A group of ants is called a 'colony'.

Poo Fact

Ants live in underground colonies with rooms for specific tasks. They even have chambers for pooing in. This prevents the poo from several thousand ants filling up the tunnels.

Beetle

There are over 4,000 types of beetle in the UK. The stag beetle is the biggest beetle in Britain. It can grow to 7.5 cm long and, while being harmless to humans, has scary-looking pincers. Beetles eat a variety of things, such as plants, pollen, nectar, other insects, and poo. A lot of beetles have wings, so they could have gone into the flying section of this book. They also have a hard shell to protect them from predators.

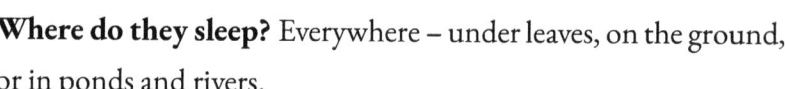

Would you like to have a hard, protective shell? (A bit like a knight's armour.)

Where do they sleep? Everywhere – under leaves, on the ground, or in ponds and rivers.

When are they active? It depends on the species; some sleep at night, some in the day.

What do they eat? Plants, pollen, nectar, other insects, dead animals, fungi, and...poo!

How long do they live for? Depending on the species, it can be a couple of months to 3 years.

How are they born? Beetles lay their eggs in rotting plants or animal poo, which provides the larvae (their young that have not yet grown into their proper shape) with something to eat once they are born.

What are they useful for? Some beetles eat insects, making them a gardener's friend; others remove dead plants and poo from the garden by eating them. Some pollinate flowers.

Miscellaneous: Beetles can both destroy and help the environment, as some species eat crops.

Collective noun: A group of beetles is called a 'colony' or a 'swarm'.

Poo Fact

Some Australian dung beetles will roll a ball of animal poo up to 200 meters to hide it in their tunnel.

Centipede

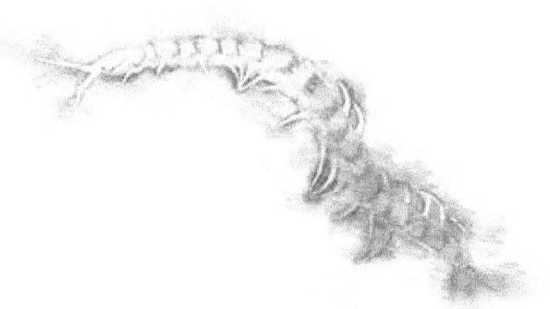

There are about 57 varieties of centipede in the UK, all of which have an odd number of legs, ranging from 15 to 101. They have one pair of legs per segment of the body, and their legs are shorter at the front than the back. As the centipedes cannot see very well, they use their two front antennae to sense the world around them.

If you had 100 legs, how would you get your trousers on?

Where do they sleep? In the soil or under logs and rocks, hidden from creatures that may eat them.

When are they active? Mainly at night.

What do they eat? Insects and worms.

How long do they live for? 5–6 years.

How are they born? Centipedes lay 30–35 eggs in the soil or a hollow in a tree. It takes 1–2 weeks for them to hatch and 2–3 years for the young centipedes to become adults. During that time, they will shed their skin on numerous occasions, also growing an extra pair of legs as they do so. Some species will guard their eggs until they hatch.

What are they useful for? They eat bugs.

Miscellaneous: Centipedes were around 400 million years ago. We may think of them as insects, but they are arthropods, which means they have no spine, have jointed limbs, and a segmented body with an exoskeleton made of chitin (like your fingernails).

Collective noun: There is no group name for centipedes. Can you think of one?

Random Poo Fact
Birds wee and poop at the same time

Millipede

There are 50 species of millipede in the UK. They can be flat looking like centipedes or tubular and can grow up to 40 cm long. Because of their weak mouths, millipedes typically feed on dead plants, although they may occasionally eat root vegetables if a slug has already eaten through the tough outer layer. Unlike centipedes, millipedes have two sets of legs per body segment. UK millipedes usually have between 40 and 400 legs.

Can you imagine how long it would take to put your shoes on if you had 400 legs?

Where do they sleep? In the soil or under logs and rocks, hidden from creatures that may eat them.

When are they active? At night.

What do they eat? Decaying plants.

How long do they live for? 7–10 years.

How are they born? They lay eggs like centipedes, and each time they shed their skin, they grow an extra pair of legs. Some species will guard the eggs until they hatch.

What are they useful for? They turn decaying plants into plant-friendly poo.

Miscellaneous: Some millipedes can emit a foul-smelling liquid to deter predators.

Collective noun: There is no group name for millipedes. Can you think of one?

Random Poo Fact
Wombats' poo is cube-shaped.

Spider

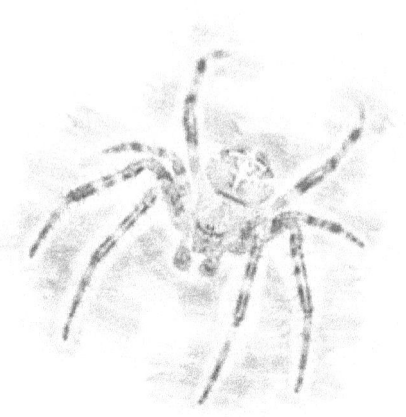

There are 650 species of spider in the UK, and they all have 8 eyes and 8 legs. Spiders are a gardener's friend as they eat a lot of bugs. You may be interested to know that not all spiders create webs. Most spiders will use the silk they create to wrap up a trapped insect, and they weave a protective pouch for their eggs. Some cast a long strand into the wind and float on it in search of a new feeding ground.

> Would you want your bedroom to be a huge web? It would be a bit like sleeping in a hammock.

Where do they sleep? Near their web, waiting for an insect to get caught in their sticky threads.

When are they active? Spiders have rest periods, but they cannot close their eyes to sleep.

What do they eat? Insects.

How long do they live for? Normally for 1 year, but some females can last up to 3 years.

How are they born? Spiders lay eggs and store them in a gossamer sack (made from their silk thread).

What are they useful for? They eat lots of insects.

Miscellaneous: Some spiders hibernate over winter. Spiders will eat old strands of their web to reuse it.

Collective noun: A group of spiders is called a 'cluster' or a 'clutter'.

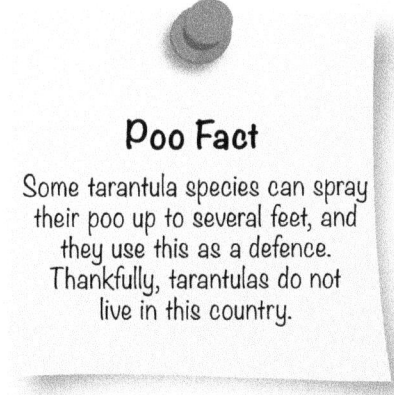

Poo Fact

Some tarantula species can spray their poo up to several feet, and they use this as a defence. Thankfully, tarantulas do not live in this country.

Slimies

Slug

Slugs and snails are related to one another. There are over 40 types of slug in the UK. Their slime is scented so the slug can find its way home. The slime also absorbs water, which is why it can be difficult to wash off your hands. Slugs can have up to 27,000 teeth and eat 40 times their weight per day.

If you had 27,000 teeth, how long would it take you to brush them?

Where do they sleep? Undercover in a damp environment, away from predators.

When are they active? Like snails, slugs prefer to come out at night. Sometimes, if it is raining with plenty of cloud cover, they will venture out in the daytime.

What do they eat? Plants and insects.

How long do they live for? Up to 2 years.

How are they born? A slug will lay up to 100 eggs at once. Slug eggs can lie dormant for years, hatching when conditions are suitable.

What are they useful for? They eat a lot of bugs. A lot of birds and animals eat them.

Miscellaneous: Slugs and snails are gastropods, which literally means 'stomach foot'. Slugs can stretch 20 times their normal length to reach food. They have green blood.

Collective noun: A group of slugs is called a 'herd'.

Poo Fact

Slugs love to eat dog poo.

Snail

There are 120 types of snail in the UK. Some are as tiny as a grain of rice. Snails are not a gardener's friend, as most of them eat plants and can destroy seedlings. Some are good for the garden, as they eat bugs and slugs.

> Would you be happy carrying your house on your back?

Where do they sleep? Undercover in a damp environment, away from predators.

When are they active? Most prefer to come out at night. Sometimes, if it is raining with plenty of cloud cover, they will venture out during the day.

What do they eat? Most eat plants, but some are carnivores. Snails will eat insects and slugs.

How long do they live for? 2–5 years.

How are they born? A snail will lay about 80 eggs at once. These eggs will hatch in about 28 days; they have soft shells, which firm up and grow with the snail.

What are they useful for? They attract birds and hedgehogs.

Miscellaneous: A snail can hibernate for up to 3 years, and they have between 14,000 and 20,000 teeth. The French cook and eat snails.

Collective noun: A group of snails is called an 'escargatoire'.

Poo Fact
Snails poo in their shell and push it out through a small hole.

Snake

We have 3 snake species in the UK, and UK law protects them. They are the smooth snake, the adder, and the grass snake. The grass snake is the one you are more likely to see in your garden and, thankfully, is not venomous. They like the heat generated by compost heaps. The grass snake will lay eggs in autumn and hibernate over winter.

Would you like to slither everywhere on your belly?

Where do they sleep? Underground or in compost heaps for warmth.

When are they active? Grass snakes are nocturnal; they are active at night.

What do they eat? Frogs, fish, small mammals, and birds.

How long do they live for? 25 years.

How are they born? Grass snakes are the only egg-laying snake native to the UK. They lay up to 40 eggs per session.

What are they useful for? They eat a wide range of pests, such as slugs and mice.

Miscellaneous: Snakes smell with their tongues. The adder is the UK's only venomous snake. It is really shy and will retreat if approached.

Collective noun: A group of grass snakes is called a 'den' or a 'slither'.

Poo Fact
If an animal attacks a grass snake, it often poos on the attacker and plays dead.

Worm

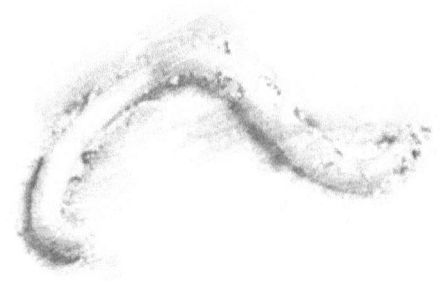

Worms are fantastic for the garden; they dig tunnels that help the rainwater soak away. Worms pull plant matter (rotting leaves and such) into these tunnels. Their poo is the basis for soil. Worm poo is one of the best and most expensive manures for the garden. You may have seen tiny cones of soil on the lawn; that's from worms.

Gardeners often farm worms in wormeries for their poo. The worms can turn plant matter into plant food much faster than a compost heap.

> Would you like to sleep underground?

Where do they sleep? Underground in their burrows.

When are they active? All the time.

What do they eat? Plant matter.

How long do they live for? Deep-burrowing worms can live up to 10 years; others live for 3–5 years.

How are they born? Worms shed cocoons that contain up to 20 eggs. If the ground is too dry, the eggs will remain dormant (like being asleep). The baby worms can take 2–11 weeks to hatch.

What are they useful for? They improve the condition of the soil, and their poo is the best plant food. Lots of creatures eat worms.

Miscellaneous: Did you know if a worm is cut in half, the head section may survive by growing a new body?

Collective noun: A group of worms is called a 'clew'.

Poo Fact
A single tablespoon of worm poo (called vermicast) can feed a small pot plant for 2 months with nutrients essential for growth.

Winged

Bat

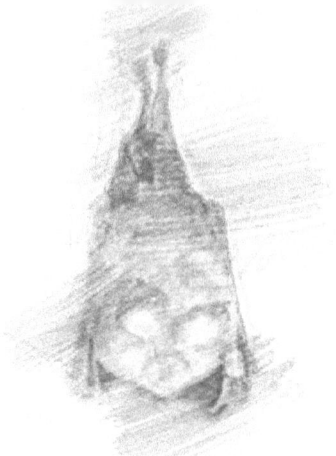

People often fear bats, but they are really cute little creatures once you get to know them. In the UK, we have 17 different species of bat, and they all sleep hanging upside down. They fly at night and rely on a combination of sight and hearing to find their way around. They emit high-pitched screeches that we cannot hear while listening to the echoes to locate obstacles and food.

Would you like to sleep hanging upside down from the ceiling?

Where do they sleep? Depending on the species, bats will hang upside down in attics, barns, caves, bat boxes, and trees.

When are they active? From sunset to sunrise; bats have excellent eyesight.

What do they eat? Insects.

How long do they live for? Different species of bats vary. Some live up to 5 years and some up to 30 years.

How are they born? Like humans, bat mothers usually have one offspring and provide them with milk until they can consume proper food.

What are they useful for? They eat a lot of pesky bugs and pollinate plants.

Miscellaneous: Bats sleep during the winter months (hibernate).

Collective noun: A group of bats is called a 'colony'.

Question: Would you like to sleep hanging upside down from the ceiling?

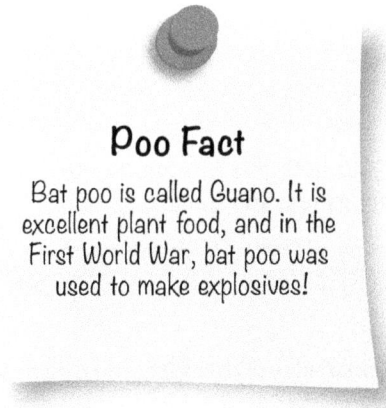

Poo Fact
Bat poo is called Guano. It is excellent plant food, and in the First World War, bat poo was used to make explosives!

Bee

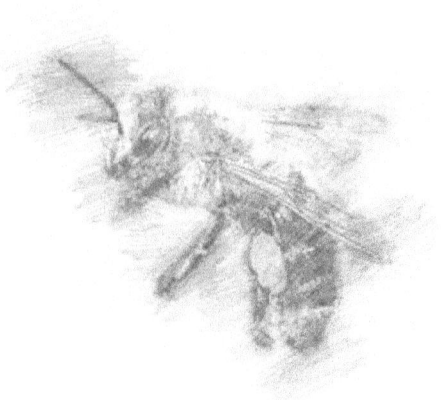

In the UK, we have over 250 species of bee, from solitary bees to bees that live in huge colonies. Bees are important pollinators; without them, our crops would not grow fruit, and we would starve. Bees can sting, but they know it will kill them to do so. On the whole, bees are calm, placid creatures. It takes 12 honeybees, who will visit 336,000 flowers during their short lives, to make one teaspoon of honey. Honeybees describe the location of flowers to the other through a bum-wiggling dance called the waggle dance.

Could you give directions by performing the waggle dance?

Where do they sleep? Honeybees live in large nests or hives, while other bees live underground, in holes in wood, and some will even sleep in the flowers!

When are they active? Daytime, preferably when it is warm.

What do they eat? Pollen and nectar from flowers.

How long do they live for? A honeybee can live for 3–25 weeks. A queen can live for 2–3 years. Wild bees live for 4–12 weeks.

How are they born? Bees lay eggs in prepared cells. In a honey hive, worker bees will look after the young. In the wild, some of the bee species leave food for the emerging bees, knowing they will not be around when they emerge.

What are they useful for? We would not have crops if we did not have bees to pollinate the flowers.

Miscellaneous: In a hive, male bees are called drones, females are worker bees, and a queen can lay 800,000 eggs in her lifetime. Bees have 5 eyes and can fly 12–20 mph.

Collective noun: A group of bees is called a 'colony' or a 'swarm'.

Poo Fact

Honeybees will not poo in the hive. During winter, they will wait and wait until it is warm enough to leave the hive.

Blackbird

Blackbirds are another favourite of the British garden and are members of the thrush family. The males are black with yellow beaks; the females are brown. They are a woodland bird that has become comfortable in town gardens.

> Would you like to go to sleep, leaving half of your brain awake? Maybe do your homework in your sleep?

Where do they sleep? In trees and bushes.

When are they active? Blackbirds are active in the daytime and the morning/evening dusk.

What do they eat? Blackbirds prefer to eat low down to the ground. They may ignore your bird feeder. They eat insects, berries, worms, spiders, and seeds.

How long do they live for? 4 years on average, but the oldest known is 21 years.

How are they born? Blackbirds lay their 3–5 eggs in their nest. The eggs are blue with a few brown speckles. Hatching after 12–14 days, the chicks leave the nest after another 12–14 days.

What are they useful for? They eat lots of bugs.

Miscellaneous: Blackbirds are one of the few creatures that puts half of their brain to sleep while the other half is awake and looking out for predators.

Collective noun: A group of blackbirds is called a 'cloud'.

Random Poo Fact
Elephants poo 50 kg a day, and it contains a lot of plant fibre. Once cleaned, it can be made into paper.

Butterfly

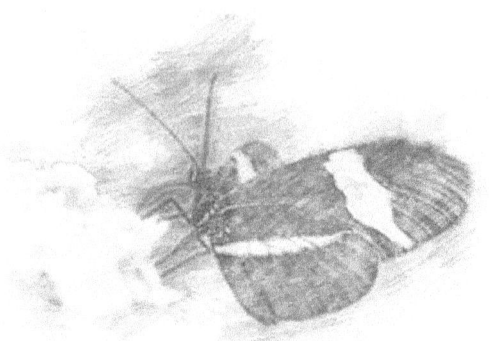

There are about 59 species of butterfly in the UK, the orange-and-black painted lady being the most common. There are about 24,000 species worldwide. Most of our butterflies die before winter, although some migrate abroad and some hibernate. As a caterpillar, a lot of gardeners think of them as a pest, as they eat plants. Butterflies are pollinators and, therefore, very important for the garden. Different species of caterpillar prefer different plants.

How would you feel if you fell asleep and woke up with wings?

Where do they sleep? They rest on the underside of leaves, often in groups.

When are they active? During the daytime when it is warm. On a warm day, you will often see a butterfly sunbathing on a rock; they are, in fact, warming up to enable them to fly.

What do they eat? Butterflies do not have teeth. Part of their mouth acts like a straw, allowing them to sip at nectar. As caterpillars, they eat plants.

How long do they live for? They spend 2–4 weeks as a caterpillar, another 2 weeks changing into a butterfly, and then their lifespan varies according to the species. Some butterflies will live for a couple of weeks, while the painted lady can live for up to 12 months.

How are they born? Butterflies lay their eggs on plants to provide the emerging babies (caterpillars) with food.

What are they useful for? Butterflies are pollinators; a large variety of creatures feast upon them and their young.

Miscellaneous: Some butterflies can taste if a leaf is suitable through their feet.

Collective noun: A group of butterflies is called a 'flutter'.

Poo Fact
When resting, the comma butterfly is disguised to look like bird poo.

Corvid

There are 8 species of bird in the corvid family, sometimes called the crow family. They are choughs, crows, jackdaws, jays, magpies, nutcrackers, rooks, ravens, and treepies. All corvids show intelligence and will use tools such as twigs to get food.

> Would you want to eat a Corvid's diet or go for a pizza?

Where do they sleep? They will roost in groups, normally in trees.

When are they active? Daytime.

What do they eat? Corvids will eat most things, including dead animals, grains, and insects. They will also steal and eat eggs from other birds.

How long do they live for? On average, they will live for 3–5 years. The oldest known was 21 years.

How are they born? Corvids lay 2–6 eggs in a large nest. Hatching after around 2 weeks, the chicks will leave the nest after 4 weeks.

What are they useful for? Members of the corvid family will eat dead animals and garbage.

Miscellaneous: Ravens can mimic human voices and electronic sounds; they will also point at something they want. This is a rare skill only observed in humans and apes. The corvid family has an excellent memory for faces and people who are kind to them.

Collective noun: A group of crows is called a 'murder' or 'parliament'. A group of magpies is a 'mischief' or 'tribe'. A group of rooks is a 'congregation' or 'parliament'.

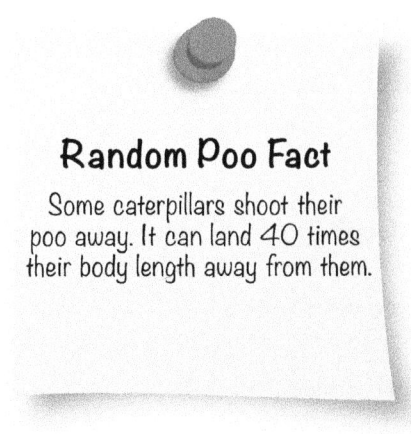

Random Poo Fact

Some caterpillars shoot their poo away. It can land 40 times their body length away from them.

Damselfly

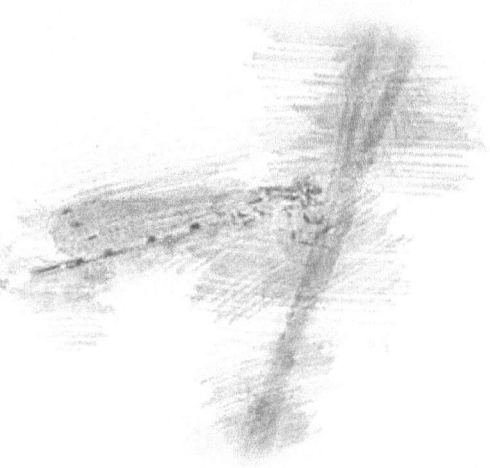

These are often mistaken for dragonflies, the damselfly, is thinner, and more delicate looking. Like the dragonfly and mayfly, they prefer wetland habitats, such as ponds and rivers. There are around 17 species in the UK.

Similar to the mayfly, damselflies fold their wings along their body when resting. Their eyes are much smaller than a dragonfly's.

> Hold your arms out like wings. That's how big the damselfly used to be. How cool is that?

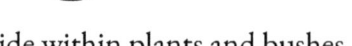

Where do they sleep? They will hide within plants and bushes.

When are they active? Daytime.

What do they eat? Insects.

How long do they live for? They can live for 2 years as water-based larvae. As a flying adult, they can live up to 3 months.

How are they born? Damselflies lay their eggs in or on aquatic plants.

What are they useful for? They eat a lot of insects, and they are, in turn, eaten by larger predators.

Miscellaneous: Some extinct forms of damselfly were nearly a meter in length.

Collective noun: A group of damselflies is called a 'swarm'.

Random Poo Fact

People buy tiger poo to protect their garden. The strong scent of the large predator will scare cats away.

Dragonfly

Dragonflies are truly beautiful creatures, and there are about 25 species native to the UK. They are easily spooked, so if you see one, stay still or it will fly away. Some people fear these timid creatures, and for no reason, as they will not attack you. They prefer to live around ponds and lakes, where they spend the first two years of their life as swimming larvae, called nymphs. When resting, a dragonfly will keep its wings outstretched. Dragonflies were flying around long before the dinosaurs roamed the planet.

How big would your sunglasses be if you had 28,000 eyes?

Where do they sleep? Hidden in bushes or under leaves.

When are they active? Daytime.

What do they eat? They normally eat midges and mosquitoes, but they will also snack on butterflies and moths.

How long do they live for? In the UK, flying adults only live for about 4 months.

How are they born? A dragonfly will attach her eggs to the stems of underwater plants.

What are they useful for? They eat a lot of pesky insects.

Miscellaneous: The eyes of a dragonfly are so large that they take up most of the space on the head. Each eye is actually a cluster of 28,000 eyes. Because of these large eyes, they have incredible vision. As nymphs in a pond, they propel themselves by shooting water from their bums.

Collective noun: A group of dragonflies is called a 'swarm'.

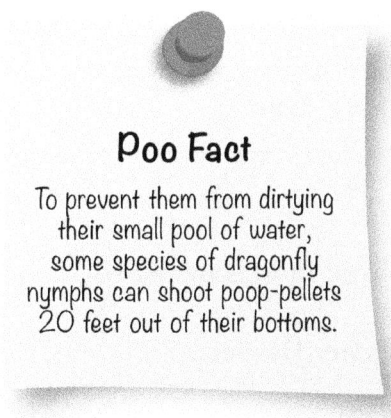

Poo Fact

To prevent them from dirtying their small pool of water, some species of dragonfly nymphs can shoot poop-pellets 20 feet out of their bottoms.

Dunnock

Dunnocks are small brown and grey birds; they are shy and will creep along the edge of flower beds and bushes, looking for food on the ground. Like wrens, they are often mistaken for sparrows. They have thin beaks, whereas the sparrow's is much thicker. Cuckoos are famous for laying their eggs in other birds' nests for them to look after the eggs and chicks, and they favour dunnock nests. Once the cuckoo chick has hatched, it will push any dunnock eggs and chicks out of the nest.

The dunnock has a nickname. What's yours?

Where do they sleep? In trees and bushes.

When are they active? Daytime.

What do they eat? Insects, berries, worms, spiders, and seeds.

How long do they live for? 2 years on average, but the oldest known is 10 years.

How are they born? Dunnocks lay 4–5 eggs in their nest, hatching after 10–12 days. The chicks leave the nest after 10–12 days.

What are they useful for? They eat lots of bugs.

Miscellaneous: The dunnock has the nickname of 'hedge sparrow'. Their eggs are light blue.

Collective noun: A group of dunnocks is called a 'jovial'.

Random Poo Fact
Dogs love to roll in smelly fox poo.

Fly

Flies are probably the dirtiest creature you will encounter in the garden. They love to feast on rotting dead animals—the smellier, the better. They also eat dog poo, and then they will happily walk over your food with bits of poo and dead animal on their feet, Gross! Flies do not have teeth, so they have to vomit on their food to make it soft enough to suck up. Yuck!

> Would you like to taste your food with your feet?

Where do they sleep? Under leaves, rocks, or somewhere that provides shelter.

When are they active? Daytime.

What do they eat? Decaying plants, dead animals, and poo. Female horseflies drink blood.

How long do they live for? Adult flies typically live for 60–90 days.

How are they born? A fly will lay 75–150 eggs in a warm, moist place, usually on food waste, a dead animal, or poo. They take 8–48 hours to hatch into maggots, depending on species, and 3–4 weeks for the maggots to change into flies.

What are they useful for? Flies eat rotting plants or dead animals and poo (yuck!); without them, there would be piles of disgusting waste littering our countryside.

Miscellaneous: Flies taste with their feet. Some flies are also pollinators. The cocoa plant (chocolate) is pollinated by flies – I hope they wiped their feet first!

Collective noun: A group of flies is called a 'swarm', a 'cloud', a 'hover', or a 'plague'.

Poo Fact
On average, flies poo every 2 minutes.

Ladybird

There are over 47 species of ladybird in the UK, and everyone is a gardener's friend. Ladybirds have enormous appetites and eat a huge quantity of pesky insects such as aphids. They are so good at reducing the number of aphids that fruit farmers buy millions of ladybirds and release them near their crops. Ladybirds can be anywhere between 1 and 10 mm in size and can be different colours, but most people are familiar with the 'harlequin' species from their orange/red shell with black spots. During winter, ladybirds group together in sheltered areas.

Ladybirds are part of the beetle family, but as they are so beautiful and have wings, I have made this page for them here.

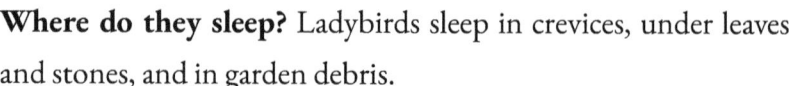

Do you think a Dalmatian would look as cute as a ladybird if it was orange with black spots?

Where do they sleep? Ladybirds sleep in crevices, under leaves and stones, and in garden debris.

When are they active? Daytime.

What do they eat? They consume huge amounts of aphids and plant-harming insects.

How long do they live for? They usually live for 1–2 years.

How are they born? Ladybirds lay their eggs near their food source.

What are they useful for? Each ladybird will eat about 50 plant-sucking aphids a day, and they are lovely little creatures.

Miscellaneous: If attacked, a ladybird will emit an unpleasant-tasting fluid. Birds associate the bright colour with the unpleasant taste and learn not to eat ladybirds again.

Collective noun: A group of ladybirds is called a 'loveliness'.

Random Poo Fact
There is a spider called the 'dung spider', as it looks like bird poo.

Mayfly

There are about 501 species of mayfly in the UK. You can often see them flying alongside a river or pond, and they are often mistaken for dragonflies. Two easy-to-spot differences between a mayfly and a dragonfly are: when resting, the mayfly folds its wings along its body, and its legs are thin and look weak. Mayflies are unique, as once they have their wings, they have two adult stages, but those stages don't last very long. Like dragonflies, there are mayfly fossils dating back over 300 million years.

If you couldn't eat, what food would you miss the most?

Where do they sleep? The adults do not really live long enough to need sleep.

When are they active? Daytime.

What do they eat? Their larvae feed on algae and plants.

How long do they live for? Depending on the species, they can live for up to 2 years as underwater nymphs. In the second stage of adulthood, they have a brief life of 1–3 days.

How are they born? Eggs are laid in water, where they will fall to the bed of the river, pond, or lake.

What are they useful for? Mayfly larvae eat smaller insects; they, in turn, are eaten by bigger predators.

Miscellaneous: Adult mayflies do not eat during their 1–3 days of life.

Collective noun: A group of mayflies is called a 'swarm'.

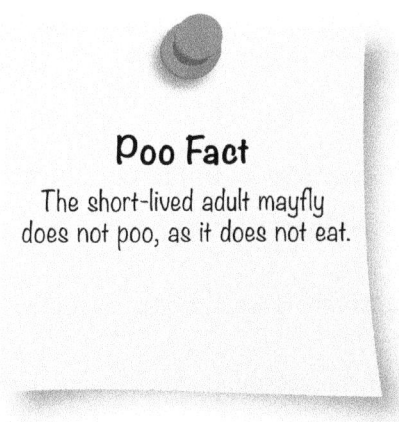

Poo Fact
The short-lived adult mayfly does not poo, as it does not eat.

Moth

Most of the 2,500 species of moth that are native to the UK look like drab butterflies. Instead of being brightly coloured, moths tend to be camouflaged, becoming almost invisible in the night-time forest. We have about 11 moths that fly about in the daytime, and they are as beautiful as butterflies.

> Would you be happy sleeping all day and going to school at night?

Where do they sleep? Moths will rest on the underside of leaves or somewhere shaded from the sun.

When are they active? Most fly about at night.

What do they eat? As caterpillars, most eat plants; as adult moths, they suck nectar. There are two species of moths that like feasting on fabric, such as cotton, wool, or leather.

How long do they live for? Most moth species spend about 50 days as a caterpillar, pupate (changing from one body shape to another) for 1–2 weeks, and then emerge as a moth for about a month. The clothes moth and the carpet moth can last up to 2 years as a caterpillar feasting on the natural fibres in your home.

How are they born? Moths lay their eggs near a food source.

What are they useful for? Most moths are pollinators. They are eaten by a wide range of creatures, such as frogs, toads, bats, and birds.

Miscellaneous: As a defence, tiger moths produce an ultrasonic clicking sound to confuse bats.

Collective noun: A group of moths is called an 'eclipse'.

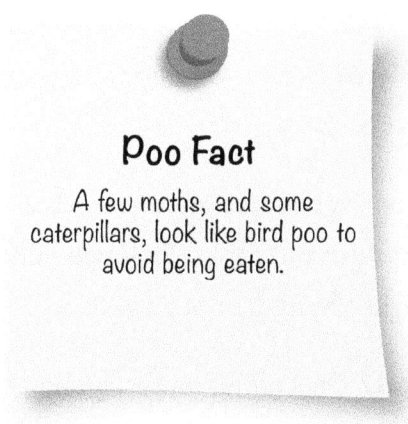

Poo Fact

A few moths, and some caterpillars, look like bird poo to avoid being eaten.

Owl

We have 4 native and 1 non-native owl in the UK: barn owl, tawny owl, long-eared owl, and short-eared owl. The little owl was introduced to our country in the 1800s.

How would you feel if you had to vomit up the bits you cannot digest?

Where do they sleep? Some owls prefer to shelter in tree hollows, while others prefer barns.

When are they active? People often see owls at night, but owls prefer to be out at dusk and dawn. They will hunt in the daytime if the previous night's hunt did not go well.

What do they eat? Depending on the species, owls will eat insects, spiders, earthworms, snails, amphibians, birds, and small mammals.

How long do they live for? On average, they will live for 4 years. In safe environments, they can live for 15 years.

How are they born? Owls lay 3–8 eggs in May, which hatch after 28–32 days. The chicks will leave the nest when they are 26–80 days old.

What are they useful for? They keep the numbers of small mammals and birds in check. If prey animals do not reduce the numbers of mice, rats, rabbits, etc., these small animals could breed faster than the food supply can support them.

Miscellaneous: Owls have excellent eyesight, but they cannot move their eyes; they have to move their heads instead.

Collective noun: A group of owls is called a 'parliament'.

Poo Fact
Owls poo, but they also produce pellets. Pellets are the bits of animals that they cannot digest, like bones and fur. These they vomit up.

Pigeon

There are five types of pigeon native to the UK: wood pigeons, collared doves, stock doves, turtle doves, and rock doves. The wood pigeon is the most common large wild bird in Britain. Many people consider pigeons to be flying vermin, as they carry a variety of diseases, even more than rats. There are also feral pigeons, those that escaped from racing pigeon trainers and breeders.

Would you want a built-in compass so you could find your way home?

Where do they sleep? Pigeons prefer a flat surface; doves will sleep in trees and bushes.

When are they active? Daytime.

What do they eat? Fruits, berries, seeds, plants, and sometimes insects.

How long do they live for? The oldest known pigeon was 16 years old, although most only live up to 3 years because of predators.

How are they born? The pigeon normally lays two eggs in their nest. It takes 17 days for eggs to hatch into baby pigeons, which are called squabs. It takes 30–35 days for the squabs to leave the nest.

What are they useful for? Pigeons breed quickly; there are lots of larger animals and birds that eat them.

Miscellaneous: Certain species of pigeon, which are used in long-distance races, can use the Earth's magnetic field to find their way home. They can fly as high as 6,000 feet and reach a speed of 77 mph.

Collective noun: A group of pigeons is called a 'band' or 'stool'.

Poo Fact
Native pigeons do not poo while flying because they would poo on their feet.

Robin

The robin is Britain's favourite small bird, partly because of the bright red patch on its chest and partly because they are friendly and cheeky. They will often join a gardener as they work the ground, swooping to pick up any disturbed bugs and worms. Robins rub ants and millipedes over their feathers, using the toxins released by these creatures to kill pesky mites and ticks. They have a lovely song too.

Do you have a cheeky robin in your garden or park?

Where do they sleep? In trees and bushes.

When are they active? Daytime.

What do they eat? Insects, berries, worms, spiders, and seeds.

How long do they live for? 2 years on average, but the oldest known is 8 years.

How are they born? Robins lay 4–6 eggs in their nest, hatching after 10–13 days. The chicks leave the nest after 10–12 days.

What are they useful for? They eat lots of bugs.

Miscellaneous: Young robins do not have red breasts. They are brown and lightly speckled. It is nearly impossible to tell female and male robins apart. Each patch of red is unique to that robin.

Collective noun: A group of robins is called a 'round'. This is unlikely to happen, as robins are solitary birds.

Random Poo Fact
Most chicks poo immediately after feeding, and the parent will remove the poo from the nest.

Sparrow

There are two types of sparrow in the UK: the house sparrow and the tree sparrow. We often group them in the 'little brown bird' category, along with dunnocks and wrens. They are one of the most common birds in the UK, though their numbers have fallen in the last 10 years. Like most birds, they have suffered because of modern farming, and plant-less gardens have removed their nesting and feeding grounds.

> If you were a bird, would you live in a hedge, bush, or tree?

Where do they sleep? In trees and bushes.

When are they active? Daytime.

What do they eat? Insects, berries, worms, spiders, and seeds.

How long do they live for? 3 years on average, but the oldest known is 12 years.

How are they born? The birds lay 2–5 eggs in their nest. They take 11–14 days to hatch. The chicks leave the nest after 14–16 days.

What are they useful for? They eat a lot of plant-eating bugs.

Miscellaneous: In 1958, the Chinese government ordered sparrows to be killed as they were eating the farmers' grain as it was growing. They killed millions of sparrows until they realised that the bugs, which the sparrows would have eaten, were now consuming far more grain and plants than the birds would have. It took a long time for the sparrow population to recover, and all the while the bugs thrived and crops suffered.

Collective noun: A group of sparrows is called a 'host'.

Random Poo Fact
Birds poo 25–50 times a day.

Starling

Some starlings fly from Northern Europe to the UK to live for the winter, as it is warmer here. Starlings are social birds and often fly in large groups, forming intricate patterns in the sky. This is called a murmuration. Starlings can look black, but under full sunlight, they have beautifully coloured feathers. They prefer to walk, rather than hop like most small birds.

Would you prefer to walk or do a boingy-hop like a small bird?

Where do they sleep? Normally in trees and bushes; in coastal areas, they will roost under piers.

When are they active? Daytime.

What do they eat? Insects, berries, worms, spiders, and seeds.

How long do they live for? 2–3 years on average, but the oldest known is 17 years.

How are they born? Preferring to nest in cavities, such as holes in trees or roofs, they lay 4–5 eggs, hatching after 12–14 days. The chicks leave the nest after 18–21 days.

What are they useful for? They eat lots of bugs.

Miscellaneous: A bright-yellow beak is an indicator of a healthy bird. They are excellent mimics, replicating other bird calls and electronic sounds.

Collective noun: A group of starlings is called a 'chattering' unless they are flying, then it is a murmuration.

Random Poo Fact
Dog poo was once used to help turn cow skin into leather.

Thrush

We have 6 thrush species in the UK: blackbird, song thrush, mistle thrush, redwing, fieldfare, and ring ouzel. The blackbird is the most common thrush and the ring ouzel is the rarest, as it only visits in the summer. Thrushes are later to rise than other birds, not really joining in with the dawn chorus. Farmers are not fans of thrushes, as they like to eat soft fruit such as strawberries.

> Would you like snails for your lunch? Eww! I wouldn't, even though the French eat them. Yuckity yuck!

Where do they sleep? In trees and bushes.

When are they active? Daytime.

What do they eat? Insects, berries, worms, spiders, and seeds. The song thrush also eats snails.

How long do they live for? On average, they live for 3 years. The oldest known is 11 years.

How are they born? Thrushes lay 4–6 eggs in their nest. The eggs are blue with speckles. Hatching after 12–14 days, the chicks will leave the nest after another 12–14 days.

What are they useful for? They eat lots of bugs.

Miscellaneous: If you see a pile of broken snail shells near a rock, that was probably where a song thrush had lunch.

Collective noun: A group of thrushes is called a 'skein'.

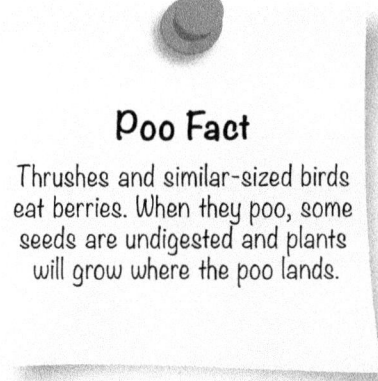

Poo Fact

Thrushes and similar-sized birds eat berries. When they poo, some seeds are undigested and plants will grow where the poo lands.

Tit

There are 6 breeding tit species in the UK. They are the blue tit, coal tit, crested tit, great tit, marsh tit, and the willow tit. Others visit the UK but breed in their own countries. Some tits, like the willow tit, are plain looking, while the blue tits are bright and colourful. Blue tits are also the most social in the family, preferring to flock in groups.

If you had to be a bird, which bird would you like to be?

Where do they sleep? Bushes and trees.

When are they active? Daytime.

What do they eat? Insects, berries, worms, spiders, nuts, and seeds. In the summer, they will feed upon pollen and nectar.

How long do they live for? 3–5 years on average, but the oldest known is 10 years.

How are they born? They prefer cavities such as holes in trees, cracks in walls, even old woodpecker nests. Tits lay 10–12 eggs in their nest, which hatch after 15–16 days. The chicks leave the nest after about 21 days.

What are they useful for? They eat lots of bugs.

Miscellaneous. When coal tits get scared, they raise their crest into small spikes, as it makes them look taller.

Collective noun: A group of tits is called a 'banditry'.

Random Poo Fact

Penguins squirt their poo out at high speed, and it can travel about 1.5 metres. Cool!

Wasp

Wasps have a terrible reputation for being nasty creatures, and unlike their calmer cousin, the bee, they can sting you as many times as they like. An aggravated wasp will spray an attacker with a scent to inform the other wasps to also sting the attacker. As horrid as they are, they play an important role in the garden, as they keep other pests under control and pollinate flowers.

> How would you feel if all your clothes were yellow and black?

Where do they sleep? Wasps chew wood to form a pulp, which they use to create nests. They do not sleep as we do, but they do have dormant periods.

When are they active? They prefer midday when it is warmest.

What do they eat? Wasps eat flies, aphids, caterpillars, other insects, and nectar.

How long do they live for? An adult worker will only live for 2–3 weeks; a queen can live as long as 1 year.

How are they born? The queen wasp lays eggs in prepared cells and workers will look after the young. It takes 4–6 weeks for an egg to grow into an adult worker.

What are they useful for? They eat a lot of bugs. They drink nectar from flowers and are also pollinators.

Miscellaneous: New wasp queens hibernate over winter before creating a nest.

Collective noun: A group of wasps is called a 'colony' or a 'swarm'.

Random Poo Fact

The most expensive coffee is made from beans that are collected from a palm civet's poo. The civet is a strange, cat-sized ammal that lives in Asia.

Wren

Wrens are tiny brown birds, and the easiest way to identify one is by its tail, which sticks upwards. Like dunnocks, they are often mistaken for sparrows. For such a small bird, they have a very loud song. Wrens are very shy and prefer to eat at ground level, darting out from bushes to retrieve food; they often ignore bird tables. Due to their tiny size, wrens struggle in harsh winters, losing up to 25% of the population.

What would you prefer for your dinner, insects, worms, or spiders?

Where do they sleep? They sleep in the safety of dense bushes. In winter, groups of up to 20 wrens can be found huddled in nest boxes for warmth.

When are they active? Daytime.

What do they eat? Insects, worms, and spiders.

How long do they live for? 2 years on average, but the oldest known is 7 years.

How are they born? They lay 5–8 eggs in a nest, which hatch after 14–17 days. The chicks leave the nest after 15–20 days.

What are they useful for? They eat a lot of bugs.

Miscellaneous: Wrens are the lightest and shortest birds found in the UK, weighing no more than a pound coin.

Collective noun: A group of wrens is called a 'herd'.

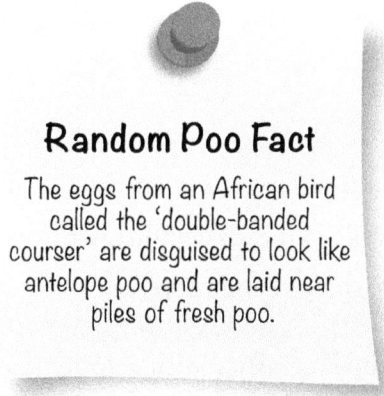

Random Poo Fact

The eggs from an African bird called the 'double-banded courser' are disguised to look like antelope poo and are laid near piles of fresh poo.

Useful Words

Here are some words you may wish to learn. They are not necessary for this book, but they will help you if you wish to learn more about the animals and insects that are all around you.

Arthropod – a spineless creature that has a segmented body and a protective shell called an exoskeleton. Arthropods include centipedes, millipedes, spiders, and more.

Amphibian – a small creature with a spine that requires water or a moist environment to survive. Amphibians include frogs and toads.

Carnivore – a creature that eats other animals. Humans are carnivorous: a beef burger comes from cows and pork sausages from pigs.

Cold-Blooded – a creature that cannot warm itself up. Cold-blooded creatures will often bask in the sun for warmth.

Crepuscular – creatures that are active during the twilight hours of dusk and dawn (the dark hour or so around sunset and sunrise).

Fledgling – a baby bird or bat that is about to leave the nest. Many fledglings are not fully capable of full flight and fall to the ground, where the mother will take care of them until they are stronger.

Habitat – the natural environment for a creature. This could be a pond, woodland, field, etc.

Herbivore – a creature that eats plants. Humans are also herbivorous, as we eat fruit and vegetables. You do eat your sprouts, don't you?

Insectivore – a carnivorous creature that eats insects.

Invertebrate – a creature lacking a backbone/spine. Worms and slugs are a good example of invertebrates.

Larvae – the young form of an insect, especially one that will change shape as it grows into an adult.

Mammal – an animal that feeds its young with milk. Mammals include mice, hedgehogs, pigs, cows, and humans.

Manure – an organic matter that is used to feed plants. Most manure comprises animal poo or rotting plant matter from a compost heap.

Nocturnal – a creature that prefers to be active at night and sleep during the day.

Omnivore – a creature that eats animals, insects, and plants. For example, mice, pigs, and humans eat all three.

A pollinator – an insect, bird, or animal that carries pollen from the flower of one plant to another. Without this, there would be no plant reproduction; therefore, no fruits, seeds, or grains would grow. Without pollinators, our farmers would not have crops to harvest.

A predator – a creature that hunts and eats other creatures.

Pupate – when a baby insect (a larva) wraps itself up in a protective cocoon (like wrapping yourself in the duvet). Over 2–3 weeks, it will change the shape of its body and emerge as an adult. For example, a caterpillar will pupate and emerge as a butterfly.

Venomous – a creature that injects a toxin into your body. When a venomous snake bites, it injects a toxin through its fangs to stun or kill its meal.

Vertebrate – a creature that has a backbone/spine. For example, you have a spine and a skeleton.

Warm-Blooded – a creature that can warm itself. Birds and mammals are warm-blooded. This includes you.

Helping Wildlife

If you have a garden, there are many things you can do to help wildlife, and some of them do not involve spending money.

By piling rocks and sticks under your bushes, you will give the insects somewhere to live.

If you can sink an old washing-up bowl into the ground by some shrubs, this will encourage frogs and toads into your garden. If you lay a couple of old (even broken) clay pots on their sides near your little pond, it will give the frogs a safe shelter to rest in.

By adding some rocks and maybe some washed gravel into the pond, you will give the water-based insects somewhere to live. Adding a rock that sticks up out of the water will allow the birds to stand on it as they drink, and securing a couple of sticks sticking out over the edge allows any animals that fall into your pond to escape.

Now and again, you could throw your apple cores or banana skins, under the bushes to decompose. Insects and worms will enjoy turning these into compost. In small amounts, it will not cause any smells and it helps the garden. If you have a large garden, you could try to make a compost heap; lots of bugs live in these, and the compost you make will be excellent for your plants.

There are many plants to encourage bees and butterflies. If you have a friend or relative with suitable plants, you may grow another one from a green twig taken from the plant. Place the twig in a jar of water for a while to see if small roots form. If they do, you can plant this in compost for it to continue growing.

Acknowledgements

A big heartfelt thank-you goes out to my beta readers. I think this book has proven we are all still children at heart.

Thank you to:

Cath Burrows

Deb Green-Jones

Deb Murphy

Fiona Knowles-Holland

Jude Lennon

Maddy Templeman

Pauline Vickers

Sue Fellows

About the Author

Authors walk in clouds of possibilities, they talk to the ghosts of characters and sometimes these ghosts are penned into reality.

P N Burrows was born in England and raised in rural Wales. Phil has worked in a variety of roles over the years from IT Consultant to a Business Advisor. In his spare time, he loves to read and particularly enjoys crime thrillers. He also enjoys working his way through a comprehensive bucket list that he and his wife have created.

https://pnburrows.com

amazon.co.uk/P-N-Burrows/e/B01F2E4AGI/

facebook.com/pages/PN-Burrows/785593698218506

twitter.com/PNBurrows

instagram.com/pnburrows_author

goodreads.com/author/show/14854812

BOOKS BY P N BURROWS

Milton Keynes UK
Ingram Content Group UK Ltd.
UKHW050716010724
444982UK00014B/911